DATE			
FE 16 '91	NOV 27 '98		
OC 15 '92	JE 1 '99		
AP 23 '93			
SE 15 '93	JA 13 '00		
SEP 01 '95	JA 11 '08		
JUN 30 '97	OC 25 '12		
AUG 14 '97	JE 05 '13		
MAR 16 '98			
JUN 25 '98			
OCT 08 '98			

I CAN BE A

WELDER

By Dee Lillegard and Wayne Stoker

Prepared under the direction of Robert L. Hillerich, Ph.D.

With special thanks to George Colville and the George Colville Welding Collection at Laney Community College, Oakland, California.

CP CHILDRENS PRESS ®

CHICAGO

Library of Congress Cataloging in Publication Data

Lillegard, Dee.
  I can be a welder.

  Includes index.
  Summary: Describes the training necessary to be a
welder and the many kinds of work that they do.
  1. Welding—Vocational guidance—Juvenile literature.
[1. Welding—Vocational guidance. 2. Occupations.
3. Vocational guidance] I. Stoker, Wayne. II. Title.
TS227.7.L55 1986   671.5'2'023   85-28995
ISBN 0-516-01895-7

PICTURE DICTIONARY

pipeline

welding booth

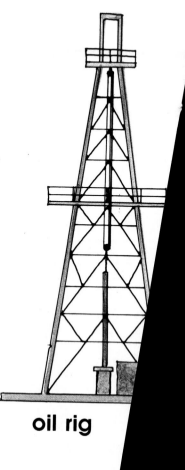

oil rig

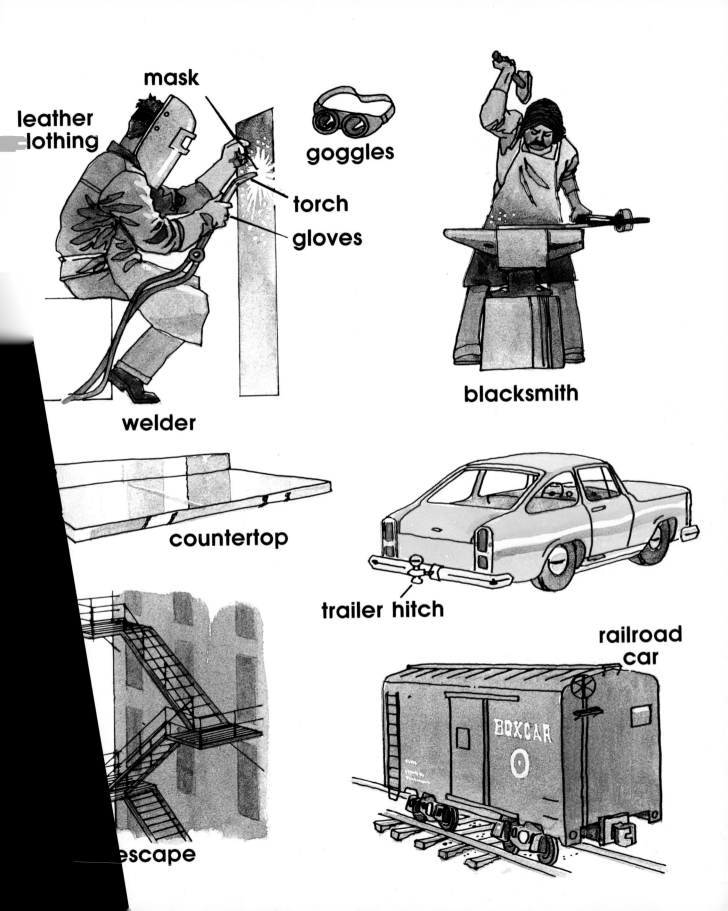

leather clothing

mask

goggles

torch

gloves

welder

blacksmith

countertop

trailer hitch

railroad car

BOXCAR

escape

Welders use gas torches or electric welding tools
to melt metals so they can be joined together.

Can you make two pieces of metal stick together? That's what welders do. They melt metals and join them together.

welder

Welders join metals to make buildings, bridges, airplanes, and many other structures.

Look at your bicycle. It
is made of pieces of
pipe welded together.

An oil pipeline is
thousands of miles

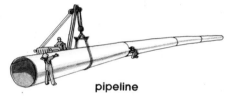

pipeline

long. It cannot be
made in one piece. By
welding many smaller
pipes together, welders
can make one long
pipe.

Welders go to school
to learn about different
metals. They learn how
metals can be joined,
or fused. They learn to
use a welding rod to
weld a joint.

Welding students
spend many hours

Welding students learning their trade

Student welders learn early in their training to
wear protective clothing and goggles for safety.

practicing in their welding booths. They begin by welding small pieces of metal together. Teachers check their welds. They make sure the welds are strong and even.

welding booth

Arc welding

There are different ways to weld. Arc welding is the best way to fuse most metals. Arc welders use electricity to make metals very hot—as hot as 7500 degrees Fahrenheit.

Gas welding

(One hundred degrees
Fahrenheit is a hot day!)
  Welders also learn
about gas, or flame,
welding. They learn to
use a torch. There are
different kinds of torches
for melting metal.

torch

13

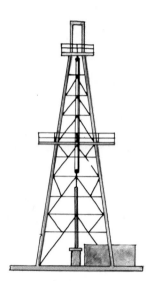

oil rig

Welders work in many different locations. They work underground, building tunnels or pipelines. They work high in the air on tall buildings. They may even work underwater on bridges and oil rigs. Welders will also be needed to build space stations in outer space someday.

High in the sky or down on the ocean floor, welders work wherever they are needed. An underwater welder uses a special torch to melt metals in water.

Welders must be
healthy and must be
good with their hands.
They must have good
hand-eye coordination.
Welders must be
careful when they work.
They have to wear

special goggles to
protect their eyes.
Welders wear masks,
leather clothing, and
gloves, too. These
protect them from
sparks of melted, or
molten, metal.

mask

leather
clothing

goggles

gloves

Left: Welder repairing a ship. Right: A team of welders welding the rudder of an enormous ship

Welders often work in teams. This is very important in shipbuilding. Each welder must weld at the right time. And each weld must be strong. The ship will only be as strong as its welds.

Welders work together with other tradespeople. They work with pipefitters, boilermakers, ironworkers, and machinists. Welders must be able to cooperate with different kinds of workers.

Blacksmiths heat metal in a furnace, or forge, and hammer it into shape on an iron block, or anvil.

The first welders were blacksmiths. Over two thousand years ago, blacksmiths were heating metals and hammering them together to join them. Their welds were not as strong as welds made today with modern equipment. They came apart easily.

blacksmith

Modern welding is less than a hundred years old. Modern welds, if done properly, will hardly ever break. Every day, welders are learning new and better ways to weld.

Some assembly plants use robot welders. But robots can never

These robot welders are working on an automobile assembly line.

replace human welders. Welders can work in places where robots cannot go. They can do things that robots cannot do.

Repairing a railroad car

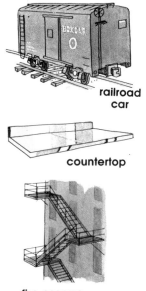

trailer hitch

railroad car

countertop

fire escape

Welders are needed for building and repairing all things made of metal. Welders make railroad cars and trailer hitches. They make fire escapes and countertops. The

Woman welders at a truck factory

stainless steel counters
you see in fast-food
restaurants are very
smooth. They must be
welded so you can't
see where the pieces
go together.

Almost any metal structure you see was built with the help of welders.

Metal is all around us—in cars, airplanes, buildings, bridges, playground equipment, and even some of your toys. Welders must always try to do a good job. The safety and lives of many people may depend on their work.

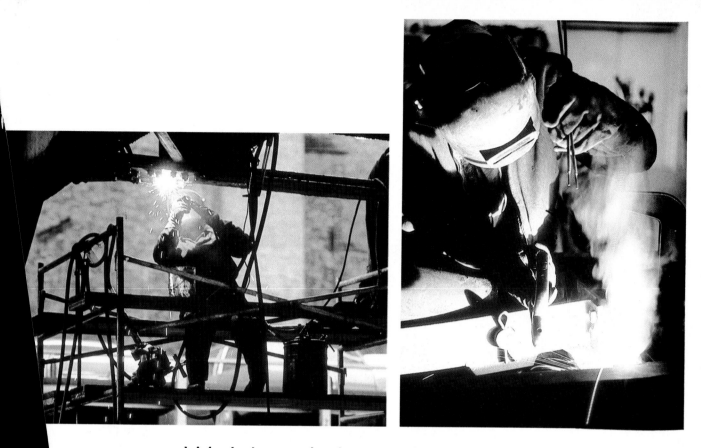

Welders take pride in what they do. They know how important their work is. Would you like to have a job that is so important? Would you like to be a welder?

WORDS YOU SHOULD KNOW

arc welding (ARK WELD • ing)—joining metals with heat produced by electricity

blacksmith (BLACK • smith)—a worker who melts and shapes metals using fire and a hammer

boilermaker (BOY • ler • make • er)—a worker who makes or repairs steam generators and water heaters

fuse (FYOOZ)—to join or blend together

gas welding (GAS WELD • ing)—joining metals with the heat of a gas torch

goggles (GOG • els)—special eyeglasses that welders wear to cover and protect their eyes from sparks

hand-eye coordination (HAND EYE coh • or • din • AY • shun)—the ability of a person's hands and eyes to work together well. The person's mind receives information from the eyes and gives orders to the hands.

ironworker (EYE • ern • work • er)—a worker who melts or molds iron

machinist (muh • SHEEN • ist)—a worker who builds or repairs machinery

molten (MOLE • ten)—melted

pipefitter (PIPE • fit • er)—a worker who installs and repairs metal pipes

robot (ROH • bot)—a machine that does some jobs or actions that people ordinarily do

space station (SPAISS STAY • shun)—a man-made satellite that orbits the earth and contains a laboratory and living quarters

torch (TORCH)—a hand-held device that emits an extremely hot flame

trailer hitch (TRAY • ler HITCH)—a device for attaching a trailer to the back of a car or truck

welding rod (WELD • ing ROD)—a rod of metal that is melted into a welded joint to strengthen and fill the joint

INDEX

PHOTO CREDITS

Courtesy Airco Technical Institute: © Mike Leskiw—9 (2 photos), 10 (2 photos)

Cameramann International, Ltd.—Cover, 18 (right), 23

Hillstrom Stock Photo:
  © Art Brown—25
  © Ray F. Hillstrom, Jr.—26 (bottom), 28, 29 (left)
  © Tom McCarthy—15 (bottom)

Journalism Services:
  © Joseph Jacobson—13, 20
  © Gregory Murphey—12
  © Harry J. Przekop, Jr.—16
  © Mark Snyder—15 (top)
  © Oscar Williams—6, 24

Nawrocki Stock Photo:
  © Michael Brohm—4 (top), 17, 26 (t[...]
  © Ted Cordingley—18 (left)

© Art Pahlke—4 (bottom)

Tom Stack and Associates:
  © Gary Milburn—29 (right)

ABOUT THE AUTHORS

Dee Lillegard (born Deanna Quintel) is the author of over two hundred published stories, poems, and puzzles for children, plus *Word Skills*, a series of high-interest grammar worktexts, and *September to September*, *Poems for All Year 'Round*, a teacher resource. Ms. Lillegard has also worked as a children's book editor and teaches writing for children in the San Francisco Bay Area. She is a native Californian.

Wayne McMurray Stoker is a Culinary Arts instructor at Laney Community College in Oakland, California. A tradesman at heart, he has been involved in the building and manufacturing trades all his life and cannot resist exploring what makes things work. Having spent his early childhood in the rural South, where storytelling was a natural pastime, Mr. Stoker finds writing for children to be an enjoyable extension of his widel[y] varied experience.